Are You Ready?

ONLY PROMISE ONCE YOU READ THIS!

ALEXANDER O. EMOGHENE

Copyright © 2024 Alexander O. Emoghene.

All rights reserved. No part of this book may be reproduced, stored, or transmitted by any means—whether auditory, graphic, mechanical, or electronic—without written permission of both publisher and author, except in the case of brief excerpts used in critical articles and reviews. Unauthorized reproduction of any part of this work is illegal and is punishable by law.

Contents

Introduction v
Prologue ix

1 Financial Transparency 1
2 Equal Contribution 9
3 Career Support 15
4 Personal Space 21
5 Family Planning 33
6 Lifestyle Changes 43
7 Communication 49
8 Support During Tough Times 55
9 Respecting Boundaries 61
10 Shared Goals 67

Epilogue 73

Introduction

I find it so special to see couples who have found love in each other's eyes. They have introduced themselves from a deeper place of the heart and are very excited to move on to the next level.

At this point, serious questions begin to surface, and clarity is sought. Having sat in counselling with countless couples, whether pre-marriage or post-marriage counselling, I have seen couples move from unlearning, relearning, and learning many relevant concepts that I have chosen to set in this book.

My wife and I have been married for two decades as of the time of this writing. As with every other marriage, we have had our fair share of ups and downs, which any marriage will respectfully endure as long as we continue to live under the sun. Some of these experiences stir my godly emotion to help the next generation of prospective marriages and intending couples hoping to tie the knot someday.

This book contains relevant solutions that can be best discussed and applied when there is still excitement between you and no clouds or gloomy days. However, this content will also benefit couples who desire transparency and healing. So, I alluded to the point where couples are ready to move on to the next. Well, it is imperative to state how tricky this stage can be because, at this point, couples get very progressive with each other's ability and commitment. There is also a tendency for couples to shun all other advice as unfavourable and prying. They seem to see each other as flawless or judge their ability in the most progressive light. That is why I ask the question on the cover: **"Are you ready? Only promise once you read this!**

In the moment's excitement, couples tend to make many promises from a cloudy, filtered place of assumptions and presumptions. However, for many, these promises do not come from a deceptive place. Because, sitting in on many counselling sessions, very few indeed come with deceptiveness, and needless to say, they soon find how challenging life can become keeping unrealistic expectations. But for the most part, the challenges that individuals may encounter are simply because of naivety and being ill-equipped to embark on the journey they excitedly set out for.

So, in this book, I aim to pose familiar promises I have heard from couples and endeavour to help other couples consider their motives and methods and draw confidence in God to stand triumphant. The content in this book will bring you to a higher level in your capacity, capability, sincerity, state of personal healing, personal and professional desire, and many more.

Proverbs 11:14 NKJV Where there is no counsel, the people fall; But in the multitude of counselors there is safety.

Promises are assertive when released in strong faith. Faith is not deep hunches but walking on a profound revelation of where the word of God directs us. Counselling provides a platform for couples to receive help, better understand their honourable intentions, and gain insights into God's perspectives. This intervention can save a couple of years of guesswork, failed promises, or resentments that may result. This work may function as a counsellor at your fingertips. You may not have the opportunity to sit before a Father, spiritual Father or mentor when you propose to your beloved, as I heard recently, "when you find your flower to pluck", but you can always open these pages and glean from the wisdom compiled for years.

Prologue

SOME BIBLICAL PURPOSES OF MARRIAGE

Proverbs 24:3 NKJV states: 'Through wisdom a house is built, And by understanding, it is established; By knowledge, the rooms are filled With all precious and pleasant riches.'

DISCOVERING THE PURPOSE OF MARRIAGE

Marriage is a divine institution where the image of God is destined to be revealed. It emphasizes the complementary nature of male and female union, reflecting the distinctive yet united Godhead ('Let us make man in our image'). Through marriage, the image of God is progressively revealed. It showcases the harmonious partnership and shared responsibilities inherent in the divine nature.

As couples anticipate the sacred covenant of marriage, it becomes imperative for them to anchor their union upon these foundational purposes. To cultivate a lasting and meaningful relationship, they must delve into the depths of God's Word, seeking divine guidance and wisdom as they set forth on the noble journey of establishing a wholesome home of abundant health and prosperity.

MARRIAGE ACTIVATES A PLACE OF TRUE WORSHIP

Marriage provides a sacred space where couples can worship and revere God. Just as Adam and Eve walked with God in the Garden of Eden, couples can cultivate an atmosphere of spiritual intimacy and connection, honouring God as the foundation of their union

(Genesis 2:15). In the sanctified embrace of marriage; couples are granted a sacred space by God, where they can intimately express their love and adoration for each other without reservation or fear. Profound revelations unfold within this holy union, revealing the essence of living following divine principles.

However, it's crucial to recognize that amidst the abundance of affection and worship exchanged between spouses, there exists a potential pitfall. When reverence for each other supersedes submission to God and His principles, the authenticity of prayer becomes distorted, veering into falsehood. Therefore, while marriage offers a unique platform for couples to exalt

Marriage provides a sacred space where couples can worship and revere God each other with reverence and devotion, it is essential to anchor their union in alignment with God's divine guidance. By prioritizing obedience to His principles, couples ensure that their worship within the marital bond remains pure and genuine, reflecting the sacredness of their commitment to God.

MARRIAGE EMPOWERS TO DISCOVER THE TRUE REVELATION OF GOD:

Through the journey of marriage, couples have the opportunity to deepen their understanding of God's character and His plan for their lives. As they navigate challenges and victories together, they can glean insights into God's faithfulness, love, and sovereignty (Proverbs 3:5-6). As the Scriptures resonate with the decree, 'Let us make man in our image and in His likeness,' we are reminded of the profound depth of this heavenly dialogue, culminating in the creation of man and woman.

Within the sanctified embrace of holy matrimony, the image of God finds its fullest expression, as the complementary union of male and female mirrors the divine harmony and unity within the Godhead. In this sacred merging, the couple will understand and experience the intricacies of God's character and attributes and the beauty of God's nature and characteristics, such as love, understanding, respect, and honour.

This truth resonates deeply within the chambers of my heart, for it underscores the transformative power inherent in embracing the laws of marriage. As we align our lives with these divine principles, we partake in the renewal, wherein the earth is ushered into a state of progressive restoration and redemption because the truth God created stands on the foundation of all things married and existing with each other. Thus, let us hold fast to the sacred covenant of marriage, recognizing it not only as a profound union of hearts but also as a divine instrument for advancing God's kingdom on earth.

In embracing the beauty and sanctity of marital love, we pave the way for a brighter, more harmonious world wherein the glory of God shines forth in all its splendour.

MARRIAGE IS THE ULTIMATE STIMULUS TO MAXIMIZE ONE'S POTENTIAL

Marriage serves as a catalyst for personal growth and development. As iron sharpens iron, couples can encourage and support each other in reaching their full potential individually and as a team (Ecclesiastes 4:9-12). Even as many individuals find purpose in their unmarried days, it's essential to underscore the transformative impact of marriage on one's health and wealth. Research consistently highlights how countless successful individuals attribute their marital union as a catalyst for enhanced well-being and prosperity in life—underscoring the profound significance of marriage as not only a source of emotional fulfilment but a powerful driver for personal growth, financial stability, and overall life satisfaction.

MARRIAGE HELPS ONE TO DISCOVER THE POWER OF SUBMISSION AND SERVANT LEADERSHIP

In the marital union, couples learn the beauty of mutual submission and servant leadership, mirroring Christ's sacrificial love for His church. By emulating Christ's example, spouses can cultivate an environment of humility, respect, and mutual honour (Ephesians 5:21-33).

The Apostle Paul, guided by the Holy Spirit, emphasizes in his letter to Timothy the honour and responsibility of leadership within the church. He underscores that among the criteria for such leadership is the requirement to be a faithful husband to one wife. Paul's wisdom extends to the profound principle that if a man cannot effectively lead and nurture his household, how can he be entrusted with serving in God's house?

Marriage, therefore, becomes the crucible where individuals learn the depth and essence of serving by God's divine principles. This service is not merely a duty or obligation but a profound reflection of God's nature and love. Within the sacred bond of marriage, couples bestow upon each other the highest form of honour and recognition, displaying selfless devotion and sacrificial love. This selfless commitment to serving one another reveals the true essence of God's character, manifesting in acts of compassion, humility, and unwavering devotion. (1 Timothy 3:4-5 **4** One that ruleth well his own house, having his children in subjection with all gravity; **5** (For if a man know not how to rule his own house, how shall he take care of the church of God?))

MARRIAGE IS GOD'S MESSAGE FOR SAFETY, EMOTIONAL, PHYSICAL, AND SPIRITUAL

Marriage provides a sanctuary of safety and refuge where couples can find solace and protection in each other's arms. Just as God promises to be our shelter and fortress, couples can rely on each other for emotional, physical, and spiritual support. (Psalms 91:**2 KJV**I will say of the Lord, He is my refuge and my fortress: my God; in him will I trust)

When considering health, statistics paint a compelling picture: married individuals exhibit significantly lower rates of sickness and disease than their unmarried counterparts. Moreover, they often enjoy longer and more emotionally focused lives, primarily due to the invaluable companionship within marriage's sanctity. **The presence of a constant confidant at Home serves as a cornerstone for emotional well-being, offering a supportive ear and a nurturing environment for open dialogue.**

Yet, beyond physical and emotional health lies a profound spiritual dimension inherent in the marriage covenant. God's favour resides when this covenant is honoured, infusing the union with divine grace and guidance. This spiritual aspect adds a depth of meaning and significance to the marital bond, and it is too sacred ordained by God to reveal the partnership in the Godhead. Thus, the blessings of health and longevity experienced by married individuals are not merely coincidental but manifest the divine favour bestowed upon the union.

MARRIAGE IS A COVER TO RECEIVE HEALING, REST, AND REFRESHMENT

Marriage offers a platform for healing and restoration through love and forgiveness. As couples extend grace and mercy to one another, they will create spaces where wounds facilitate the healing needed to become a power couple, and hearts are made whole (1 Peter 4:8). This purpose is deeply embedded in the very fabric of human existence, illustrated vividly in the genesis of Eve. As God performed surgery on Adam, tenderly addressing his wounds, a profound truth emerged: within humanity lies a myriad of deep-seated wounds, often elusive and intangible. These wounds encompass the profound ache of loneliness, the unspoken burden of rejection, and the weariness of navigating life's challenges alone. Indeed, in His infinite wisdom, God declared, "It is not good for man to be alone."

God unveils the blueprint for proper health and wholeness in the sacred union of marriage. Just as He healed Adam's wounds and united him with Eve, marriage embodies the epitome of divine restoration and completeness. Humanity's fragmented pieces find healing and reconciliation within this sacred bond, forging a path towards true flourishing and fulfilment.

In essence, the union of Adam and Eve serves as a timeless depiction of the holistic health and harmony that the world yearns to attain. God offers a transformative platform for restoring human brokenness through the divine institution of marriage. (Matthew 11:28-30).

Today, we are experiencing a level of despair that is not compared with the years gone by. To the extent that very young are committing suicide and all kinds of violent crimes relating to fatherlessness and homelessness. When asked, inmates usually trace their present condition to dysfunction at Home. In his wisdom, God created the Garden of Eden as a sanctuary of refreshment and rest for the first couple. This template is what marriage is all about.

Psalms 68:5-6 NKJV A father of the fatherless, a defender of widows, Is God in His holy habitation. 6 God sets the solitary in families; He brings out those bound into prosperity; But the rebellious dwell in a dry land.

MARRIAGE IS GOD'S SPIRITUAL AND LEGAL GROUND FOR PROCREATION

Children are God's heritage, so one of marriage's fundamental purposes is to procreate and build a family. As stewards of God's heritage in this life, couples nurture and raise children in the Lord's fear and admonition, passing down a legacy of faith and love to future generations (Genesis 1:28).

Perhaps the most widely recognized and practised purpose of marriage worldwide, it holds profound significance in the divine plan ordained by God Himself. Yet, amidst the prevailing acceptance of marriage, a divergence exists from its sacred essence. The reluctance to embrace the institution of marriage, opting instead for alternative relational structures, stands in stark contradiction to God's prophetic vision and divine mandate.

God's grand design extends beyond individual fulfilment to encompass the propagation of generations yet unborn (Psalms 102:18 NKJV) devoted to praising Him and fulfilling their divine destiny. However, the endorsement of non-traditional relationship structures undermines this overarching vision, unleashing spiritual turmoil and violence against the unborn. This spiritual upheaval finds manifestation in the widespread scourge of abortion, a grievous assault on the sanctity of life ordained by God.

Marriage emerges as the sacred bastion of hope and restoration to counter this insidious onslaught and realign humanity with God's divine purpose. By embracing the marriage covenant and upholding the traditional male and female family unit, humanity can thwart the forces seeking to derail God's divine plan, preserving God's vision for the future for the future, through this sacred union of marriage, in some cases, bankruptcies and His purposes ultimately fulfilled.

As couples embark on the journey of marriage, they honour and uphold these divine purposes, continuing to seek wisdom and guidance from God's Word. In conclusion, the institution of marriage encompasses profound purposes ordained by God, ranging from spiritual worship and personal growth to healing and Procreation.

Psalms68:5-6 NKJV A father of the fatherless, a defender of widows, *Is* God in His holy habitation? **6** God sets the solitary in families; He brings out those who are bound into prosperity; But the rebellious dwell in a dry *land.*

MARRIAGE IS GOD'S DIVINE ENVIRONMENT FOR TRUE NAKEDNESS

In marriage, couples experience profound intimacy that transcends physicality. It is a union where they can be fully known and accepted, stripped of pretence and vulnerability. Like Adam and Eve's nakedness in the Garden of Eden, marital intimacy reflects a deep spiritual and emotional connection (Genesis 2:25).

Have you ever wondered why couples begin to resemble one another after a while of living together? Is this mere coincidence or something more profound? Indeed, this intriguing aspect of marriage reflects the deep interconnectedness and intimate bond forged between two individuals. Within the sacred realm of marriage, individuals find solace in being entirely accepted, allowing them to unveil the depths of their hearts without fear or reservation.

Marriage transcends the realm of uncertainty, providing a sanctuary where couples can lay bare their vulnerabilities, knowing that their partner will stand by them through thick and thin. In this sacred union, individuals can courageously reveal their true selves—the good, the bad, and the ugly—without succumbing to shame or judgment. Even as perspectives evolve, couples can navigate the winds of change with openness and resilience, drawing strength from the unwavering support and companionship they find in each other's embrace.

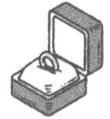

CHAPTER 1

Financial Transparency

The promise of complete financial transparency but later hides debts or overspending habits.

They promise complete financial transparency but later hide debts or overspending habits.

Financial matters must be exercised cautiously in marriage relationships, as they often are a significant source of tension. Research has shown that most divorces occur for one financial reason or another.

Matters such as hiding debts or indulging in overspending habits can swiftly lead to trust issues and financial strain between partners. Couples determined to engage in open and honest discussions about finances before marriage stand a chance to address and avoid potential financial pitfalls.

Couples must disclose all debts and financial commitments to one another, including financial habits such as spending, hoarding, and ignorance surrounding financial literacy. Moreover, couples should strongly consider creating a joint budget and formulating a plan for their financial goals together. We shall delve into this further.

Seeking the guidance of a financial advisor can also prove immensely helpful. They can provide expert insight and advice on managing finances as a married couple. Couples can lay a solid foundation for a harmonious and financially stable relationship by proactively addressing financial matters early on.

When people go into marriage, they may not be aware that as they were being joined together in spirit, soul, and body, they were also joined financially. And that God also intends to use both parties as leverage to increase their potential for financial empowerment. This unawareness makes some choose financial structures that work against this promise to be financially transparent.

Hence, establishing a solid and biblical financial structure is paramount for the health and stability of a married couple. Without clear financial boundaries and agreements, strains can emerge, potentially leading to stress and discord.

Several common financial structures couples exist, but I will endorse one of the most commonly adapted options. The first option involves maintaining separate bank accounts for personal spending while contributing agreed-upon amounts to a joint account for shared expenses such as household bills and savings goals. This setup allows for financial independence while fostering collaboration in managing everyday financial responsibilities.

Alternatively, some couples may opt for complete transparency and trust, maintaining separate accounts while sharing financial information and responsibilities openly. This approach requires a high level of mutual trust and communication to ensure that both partners uphold their commitments and maintain transparency in their financial dealings.

The third option is for couples to merge their finances entirely by opening a joint account to manage all income, expenses, and savings collectively. Joint accounts firmly oppose division and disunity and signify a deep commitment and partnership in planning their financial future together.

In the spirit of the biblical teaching of two becoming one in everything, the third option, where couples choose to merge their finances entirely, aligns closely with this principle. As Christians striving to embody a profound level of love and unity within their marriage, this option holds significant value. At least you are not subconsciously practising separation from your early life together.

In any relationship, merging two lives entails the convergence of diverse backgrounds, including distinct financial histories, habits, and attitudes shaped by upbringing and past experiences.

It means to have separate purses as the married couple already set the precedent to be tempted with pride that one account looks richer, or one may become bitter or resentful because they may feel like they are an unequal contributor to household responsibilities.

By pooling all financial resources into a joint account, couples symbolically demonstrate their commitment to shared responsibility and partnership in every aspect of their lives, including economic affairs.

Embracing this third financial structure reflects a deep level of trust, selflessness, personal maturity, and sacrificial love, which are fundamental to a thriving Christian marriage. It encourages couples to prioritize the collective well-being of their family unit over individual interests, fostering a spirit of unity and harmony within the relationship.

Moreover, by entrusting their finances to each other completely, couples demonstrate a profound faith in God's provision and guidance for their lives together. They acknowledge that their union is not just a legal or emotional bond but a sacred covenant ordained by God, and they commit to navigating their financial journey together, guided by principles of stewardship, generosity, and mutual care.

LACK OF FINANCIAL TRANSPARENCY AND POSSIBLE ISSUE

In any relationship, merging two lives entails the convergence of diverse backgrounds, including distinct financial histories, habits, and attitudes shaped by upbringing and past experiences. These differences can create a complex landscape where divergent financial backgrounds intersect, potentially leading to friction and misunderstandings. That is why, during counselling, the issue of inner healing and being ready to confront the underlying problems is encouraged.

At the core of these challenges lies the fundamental importance of trust and honesty within finances. Financial matters are deeply intertwined with the fabric of trust in a relationship. When one partner conceals debts, overspending, or other economic issues, it breaches the trust that forms the bedrock of a healthy partnership. Such a lack of transparency can sow seeds of suspicion and insecurity, gradually eroding the relationship's foundation.

Moreover, financial disparities between partners can significantly influence the power dynamics within the relationship. In cases where one partner possesses more excellent financial stability or control, there is a risk of power imbalances emerging. The partner with more economic resources may wield undue influence or feel entitled to make unilateral decisions, leading to feelings of resentment and inequality within the relationship.

Conflict over spending priorities is another common manifestation of divergent financial backgrounds. Variances in economic priorities and spending habits can ignite disagreements, with one partner prioritizing saving for the future while the other leans towards immediate gratification. Many clashes stem from how money is allocated and can escalate into arguments, straining the relationship and hindering mutual understanding.

Furthermore, couples need to pray for wisdom on how to understand the importance of long-term financial planning must be recognized. Planning for significant milestones such as buying a house, starting a family, or saving for retirement necessitates mutual understanding and cooperation. If partners find themselves at odds regarding financial goals and timelines, it can breed uncertainty and tension about the relationship's trajectory.

In essence, you will hear the newly excited couple say to each other, "I love you the way you are." However, that is a half-truth because most couples end up unhappy because their spouse remains that way year in and year after their wedding.

The weight of financial stress is yet another burden that couples may face. Mounting debts, unforeseen expenses, or a lack of economic security can contribute to heightened anxiety and strain on mental well-being. Moreover, differences in how partners cope with financial stress can exacerbate tensions, further complicating the relationship landscape.

In essence, you will hear the newly excited couple say to each other, "I love you the way you are." However, that is a half-truth because most couples end up unhappy because their spouse remains that way year in and year after their wedding. So, navigating the intricacies of divergent financial backgrounds requires a delicate balance of trust, transparency, and mutual respect.

By fostering open communication and prioritizing shared financial goals, couples addressing conflicts with empathy and understanding with a strong desire for growth can overcome the challenges posed by their financial disparities and build a resilient foundation for a thriving relationship. Now, let's delve into the promises of agreeing to share household responsibility.

CHAPTER 2
Equal Contribution

They agree to share household responsibilities equally but later expect one partner to take on most of the work.

They agreed to share household responsibilities equally but expected one partner to do most of the work later.

This might be abrupt, but caution is needed. Expecting unequal contributions to household responsibilities can lead to resentment and imbalance in the relationship. However, newlywed couples often express excitement by saying things like "We shall help each other!" or "We shall do this together!" But what does this mean, and what does it look like in practice?

After the wedding, couples slowly realize this promise was not wishful thinking and begin to falter.

To delve into the complexity so that your decision is more rounded and wise, here are quick practical tools that may start you both off on a good foundation. Before you say "I do," envisage yourselves already taking responsibility.

1. Discuss each partner's expectations and capabilities regarding household chores.
2. Create a schedule or divide tasks based on individual strengths and preferences.
3. Regularly reassess and adjust the division of responsibilities as needed to ensure fairness and mutual satisfaction.

THE PROMISE

As couples embark on the journey of marriage, the promise of "Equal Contribution" in sharing household responsibilities often serves as a cornerstone of their commitment to each other. Initially, this pledge may seem fair and equitable, reflecting a shared vision of their love in partnership and cooperation. However, as time passes, various factors can contribute to feelings of resentment and imbalance, disrupting the harmony within the relationship. I am discussing this as an inevitable situation but as a heads-up to opt for healthier and more responsible choices in how you conduct your steps in marriage.

One significant factor influencing the perception of equal contribution is implicit gender expectations. Despite strides towards gender equality, deeply ingrained societal norms and expectations regarding gender roles in domestic tasks persist in many cultures. Even when couples explicitly agree to share responsibilities equally, unconscious biases and societal pressures may subconsciously influence their perceptions and behaviours. For example, one partner might still assume that specific tasks are primarily the responsibility of the other based on traditional gender roles, inadvertently leading to an uneven distribution of labour. This is where your spiritual compass should help both couples to understand the true essence of equal contribution more deeply.

What does scripture say about the role of the man or the woman? Is it merely doing the dishes, laying the bed, or vacuuming the flat? Or is it much more? All these dynamics were absent when Adam and Eve performed their roles set before them in the Garden of Eden. Yet we can enjoy seeing God call them blessed (empowered to be fortunate and happy). (Genesis 1:28) He then charged them to be fruitful, multiply and replenish the earth.

BLESSED AND EMPOWERED

Blessed means to be empowered; they are equally empowered to play their role. So, promising to be the best husband or wife without a deeper understanding of spiritual roles and assignments will only lead to resentment. Many of the Christian persuasion may still want to see equal contribution from a cultural perspective where that might be a vast gem that you can glean from; it is imperative as a couple under God to consult the Holy Scriptures; in doing so, you will find that the contribution God handed to Adam is different from the contribution God gave to Eve.

Although they were equally empowered, they were empowered for the different tasks, and this is where these age-lone disparities are felt, "yes", even for couples that are Christians. Spiritual people will end up better off keeping this promise of equal responsibility than the spiritually ignorant. Moreover, disparities in workload can also contribute to feelings of unfairness and resentment within the relationship. Partners may have differing work schedules, commitments, or energy levels, impacting their ability to contribute equally to household chores.

For instance, if one partner works longer hours or has a more demanding job, they may have less time and energy to devote to household tasks than the other partner. This imbalance in workload can create a sense of burden and frustration, particularly if one partner feels they are shouldering a disproportionate amount of responsibility.

Additionally, unspoken expectations and mismatched interpretations of what constitutes "equal contribution" can exacerbate resentment. Without clear communication and agreement on roles and responsibilities, couples may have differing perceptions of what is fair and equitable. Each partner may bring their upbringing, personal preferences, and past experiences to the table, resulting in differing expectations that can lead to tension and discord within the relationship.

Emotional labour, often overlooked but equally demanding as physical tasks, also plays a significant role in the division of household responsibilities. Tasks such as managing finances, planning events, and coordinating family affairs require considerable emotional investment and effort. If one partner consistently bears the burden of emotional labour while the other focuses solely on tangible household tasks, it can lead to feelings of imbalance and resentment over time. Couples who keep this promise of equal contribution must consistently create genuine appreciation where couples identify their partner exerting emotional labour.

Furthermore, communication breakdowns or conflict avoidance can hinder efforts to address concerns and find mutually satisfactory solutions. Couples may shy away from discussing issues or grievances due to fear of conflict or discomfort, allowing underlying tensions to fester and escalate. Without open and honest communication, bridging the gap between expectations and reality becomes challenging, exacerbating feelings of resentment and imbalance within the relationship.

In navigating these challenges, couples must prioritize clear communication, mutual understanding, and a willingness to renegotiate roles and responsibilities as needed. By fostering open dialogue, expressing a desire to pray together and praying for each other while acknowledging the influence of implicit biases and societal expectations, couples can work towards a more equitable division of household responsibilities that honours their commitment to God and each other. Through empathy, compromise, and mutual support, couples can navigate the complexities of marriage with grace and understanding, strengthening their bond and fostering a harmonious partnership built on trust and cooperation.

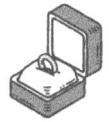

CHAPTER 3

Career Support

They promised unwavering support for each other's career ambitions but later pressure a partner to prioritize family over their career.

They promise unwavering support for each other's career ambitions but later pressure a partner to prioritize family over their career. It will be helpful to assert that this promise is very human and that its intent is rooted in the seed of destiny God placed within both genders.

Genesis 1:28 Then God blessed them and said, "Be fruitful and multiply. Fill the earth and govern it. Reign over the fish in the sea, the birds in the sky, and all the animals that scurry along the ground."

Unravelling the complexities surrounding the promises made within the context of marriage reveals profound insights rooted in the scriptures. The essence of these audacious pledges couples make to each other is often uttered in the enthusiasm of love and devotion and resonates deeply with the biblical narrative. Just as Adam and Eve were entrusted with divine purpose, empowered with unlimited resources and space for growth, and rightly empowered to support each other's dreams, so too do couples today vow unwavering support for one another's aspirations.

By divine order in creation, Adam was ordained as a leader, and Eve, endowed with the vision of an enforcer, exemplifies the complementary roles within a partnership. Each is empowered to fulfil their unique calling while bolstering the other. God designed this unique partnership, causing Adam and Eve subconsciously and naturally to thrive in divine purpose. However, often ignorance of the implications of not fully grasping this spiritual law and all that it has to help to establish a home made in heaven sets the couples up with minimal strength of agreement and, ultimately, minimal fulfilment. So, before venturing to make such bold promises, a word of caution beckons. While the scriptures illuminate the sanctity of mutual support and shared dreams within marriage, they also underscore the importance of prudence and discernment. As we tread the path of love and commitment, let us do so with eyes wide open, mindful of the responsibilities and challenges that accompany our promises.

GODLY CAUTION

Conflicting career ambitions can strain a relationship if not addressed openly and respectfully. When partners have divergent or incompatible career goals or aspirations, tension and difficulty can result if these differences are not openly acknowledged and handled with respect and appreciation. In simpler terms, it highlights potential conflicts when partners have different ideas or plans regarding their career paths. These conflicts can arise from differences in priorities, ambitions, or the amount of time and energy each partner wants to dedicate to their career pursuits.

Therefore, the promise of unwavering support for each other's career ambitions is a beautiful commitment that can significantly strengthen a relationship when understanding and prayers rule a relationship. However, despite the initial promise, various factors and dynamics within the relationship and external influences can challenge and lead one partner to prioritize family over their career.

Here are some processes that may contribute to this:

In the exhilarating journey towards marriage, couples often pledge unwavering support for each other's career aspirations. However, the practicalities of life and unforeseen circumstances can challenge fulfilling these promises. Here, we explore several factors that can hinder the realization of career support vows and offer practical solutions to navigate these complexities within a relationship.

FINANCIAL CONSIDERATIONS

Economic realities, such as the need for dual incomes or concerns about financial stability, can shape career decisions within a marriage. If one partner's career offers greater financial security for the family, they may feel compelled to prioritize it over their partner's ambitions. Couples in such a situation can engage in transparent discussions about their financial goals; if there are children, bring this heartily under your discursion and explore creative solutions to support each other's career aspirations while maintaining emotional and financial stability. Asking vital questions triggers deep conversations about each other's dreams and desires to keep them alive and not become insensitive to the couple, which has a lesser financial capacity.

PARENTAL RESPONSIBILITIES

The arrival of children profoundly impacts career trajectories, often leading one partner to prioritize caregiving responsibilities over their career ambitions. Couples can foster open communication and equitable distribution of parenting responsibilities to address this matter.

Flexibility, understanding, and grateful support from both partners are crucial in navigating the challenges of balancing career aspirations with parental duties. Communication Breakdowns: Miscommunication or unspoken expectations regarding career support can breed resentment within a relationship. Couples can avoid this by prioritizing honest and open communication about their career goals and expectations. Regular check-ins and active listening help ensure both partners feel valued and supported in their professional endeavours.

CULTURAL AND FAMILIAL PRESSURES

External influences, such as cultural norms and familial expectations, can impact career decisions and priorities within a relationship. Couples facing such pressures should maintain open dialogue and assert autonomy in career choices. By aligning their values and priorities, couples can authentically resist external pressures and support each other's career aspirations. Personal Sacrifice: Sometimes, individuals may willingly prioritize their partner's career or family needs over their ambitions out of love and devotion.

While noble, such sacrifices need a mindful state and mutual understanding. Couples can navigate these situations by fostering a culture of reciprocity and mutual support, where both partners feel empowered to pursue their professional goals while prioritizing the well-being of the family unit.

Navigating career support within the context of marriage requires couples to confront practical challenges with resilience, empathy, and proactive communication. By acknowledging the complexities of balancing career aspirations with familial responsibilities and external pressures, couples can forge a path towards mutual support and fulfilment in their personal and professional lives.

Practical Solution:

1. Discuss long-term career goals and aspirations with your partner.
2. Identify ways to support each other's professional growth while considering the impact on the relationship and family life.
3. Maintain open communication about career decisions, be willing to compromise, and find a balance that works for both partners.

CHAPTER 4

Personal Space

You agree to respect each other's personal space but later become overly clingy or controlling.

You agree to respect each other's personal space but later become overly clingy or controlling.

"I will let you be yourself," "I will give you your space," "You are free to have your quiet time." "You know I am a gentle person."

Couples often make such promises when the skies are clear and the world seems painted in hues of red roses and chirping birds. Yet, they may succumb to the temptation of becoming discourteous, disrespectful, unkind, and occasionally irritable as the uncontrollable tide of familiarity seeps into their relationship—a phenomenon we will delve into further in this chapter.

The phrase "Familiarity breeds contempt" is a proverbial wisdom suggesting that the closer we become to something or someone, the more likely we are to take them for granted or view them with less respect or admiration.

In the realm of relationships, it implies that as intimacy grows, so does the risk of overlooking boundaries, feelings, and desires, leading to a breakdown in mutual respect and understanding.

Respecting boundaries in a relationship entails agreeing to honour and uphold each other's personal space, autonomy, and preferences.

However, repeatedly crossing these boundaries without consent can gradually erode trust and respect between partners, ultimately damaging the relationship's foundation. "familiarity" comes from the Latin word "familiarities," which denotes intimacy and friendship. It also describes situations or people we know well, and it connotes close relationships and sexual intimacy.

Before exchanging vows of this nature, it is crucial to delve into the concept of familiarity and the power of intimately knowing your spouse while maintaining the fire of curiosity and discovery.

Familiarity with one's spouse can be a potent force for joy, fondness, and sexual pleasure, but it can quickly turn sour. The pledge to respect each other's personal space may soon erode due to the assumption of knowing each other too well. Scripture provides examples of how intimacy, when not approached with reverence and boundaries, can lead to separation, divorce, and even hostility.

The prime example is Lucifer, now known as Satan, who, despite his proximity to God the Father in heaven, overstepped the boundaries set between God and angels, ultimately paying the ultimate price for violating God's personal space (Isaiah 14).

Promising to respect each other's personal space is vital in any relationship, as it reflects a fundamental respect for individual autonomy, meditation, and intimacy with the spirit of God in freedom to personal worship. However, despite the best intentions, couples may struggle to uphold this promise due to various challenges.

INSECURITY AND FEAR OF LOSS

One partner may become overly clingy or controlling out of fear of losing the other person. Insecurity about the relationship's stability or fear of abandonment can lead to the desire to constantly monitor and control the partner's actions, resulting in a lack of respect for personal boundaries and space.

UNRESOLVED ATTACHMENT ISSUES

Past experiences of attachment trauma or insecure attachment styles can influence behaviour in romantic relationships. Individuals with anxious attachment styles may seek constant reassurance and validation from their partners, leading them to become overly clingy or intrusive in an attempt to alleviate their anxieties. (Philippians 3:13 KJV Brethren, I count not myself to have apprehended: but this one thing I do, forgetting those things which are behind, and reaching forth unto those things which are before.)

LACK OF SELF-AWARENESS

Some individuals may struggle to recognize or acknowledge their need for personal space and autonomy. They may mistakenly believe that constant togetherness is a sign of love and closeness, overlooking the importance of maintaining individual identities and boundaries within the relationship.

COMMUNICATION CHALLENGES

Miscommunication or unspoken expectations regarding personal space can contribute to misunderstandings and conflict in the relationship. If one partner feels suffocated or controlled by the other's behaviour but cannot express their feelings openly, it can create tension and resentment over time.

DIFFERENT NEEDS AND PREFERENCES

Couples may have different needs and preferences regarding personal space and independence. While one partner thrives on solitude, the other craves constant companionship and closeness. Balancing these differing needs can be challenging and requires compromise and understanding from both parties.

BOUNDARY VIOLATIONS

Over time, one partner may gradually encroach upon the other's personal space and boundaries without realizing it. Small gestures, such as checking their partner's phone without permission or monopolizing their time and attention, can gradually erode trust and autonomy. We shall discuss this in more detail in later chapter nine.

CODEPENDENT DYNAMICS

In codependent relationships, individuals may struggle to maintain boundaries and prioritize their needs over their partner's. They may derive their sense of self-worth and identity solely from the relationship, leading to enmeshed and controlling behaviour that stifles personal growth and interdependence.

EXTERNAL INFLUENCES

External factors such as societal pressure, family expectations, or cultural norms can also influence behaviour within the relationship. Couples may feel pressure to conform to societal ideals of romantic love or traditional gender roles, leading them to neglect their own needs for personal space and autonomy.

It reminds us that the path to the 'I Do's are paved with love and the inner work of self-discovery, healing, and growth.

"At the heart of the institution of marriage lies a fundamental truth: it is designed for individuals who have attained maturity and undergone certain levels of healing. The archetype that serves as the blueprint for the readiness required to utter the solemn vow of 'I Do' is none other than the timeless story of Adam and Eve. Embedded within the narrative of Adam and Eve's union is a profound lesson on the prerequisites for a fulfilling marriage.

Adam showed up as a full-grown man who had undergone a surgical and healing procedure. "God healed Adam's wound; Eve, on the other hand, emerged as a complete woman full of glory. So, too, must those who seek to enter into the marriage covenant, should they desire to arrive as whole and healed individuals.

This concept serves as a hallmark of the sanctity of marriage—an acknowledgement that the union of two souls is a sacred endeavour reserved for those who have attained emotional maturity and inner harmony. Like Adam and Eve, who stood as exemplars of wholeness before embarking on their journey together, through this book, I will encourage couples today to ensure they have wise counselling and mentorship to prepare them to contribute to their partnership founded on strength, understanding, and mutual respect.

Thus, the story of Adam and Eve stands as a timeless template, guiding individuals toward a deeper understanding of the profound commitment that marriage entails. It reminds us that the path to the 'I Do's are paved with love and the inner work of self-discovery, healing, and growth.

The story of Adam's creation holds profound insights into the nature and nurture of relationships. Created as a fully grown man, Adam exemplified maturity from the outset, setting a standard for those seeking companionship. A young man desiring to enter into marriage must demonstrate physical, emotional and financial maturity and a kin understanding of life's complexities.

Central to this understanding is the recognition of the need for personal space—an essential element in fostering individual growth and contributing to a relationship's overall health. Moreover, God's meticulous care in creating Adam aids our decision-making regarding getting married. As a tutorial, it challenges us to go beyond physical form and environmental space to spiritual. God imparts a crucial lesson to us as we watch him sealing Adam's wounds: relationships are best forged between whole and healed individuals. This principle underscores the inherent truth that "hurting people hurts others." By tending and healing Adam's wounds before the union with Eve, God ensures that the foundation of their relationship is built upon strength and wholeness.

In the same vein as Adam's completeness, Eve arrives as a fully formed woman, emphasizing the importance of individual healing and an already robust relationship self-awareness. Yet, even with this foundation of wholeness, the first couple encounters challenges, highlighting the inherent complexities of human connection.

Reflecting on Adam and Eve's journey prompts a sobering question: If even a couple as initially whole and healed as Adam and Eve faced difficulties, what hope is there for those who enter relationships carrying unresolved wounds and burdens? This question serves as a poignant reminder of the necessity for self-reflection, healing, growth, and trust in God's grace before embarking on the partnership journey.

HOW TO MAINTAIN A BALANCED ATTITUDE WITH YOUR PARTNER'S PERSONAL SPACE

It's essential to be respectful and mindful of their preferences. Simply saying I do at that altar does not imply that two are joint. The joint project will take place as an ongoing project.

Three types of joining take place when a couple say I do. First, the spiritual joining occurs when both couples speak at the altar. By that precious word, exchange by the couples. The vow to be with each other for the rest of your life; with that vow, the preacher pronounces both "Husband and wife". **The Second joining is when the couple consummate their marriage** (making love after the wedding ceremony). They become one in the body as one flesh because blood is exchanged, and they become one flesh with each other. **There is a third**

joining, and this is the most complex of them all because this is the progressive joining of the soul.

Marriage is understood and becomes increasingly enjoyable when soul joining is revealed to couples; this is where many may need help understanding why marriage may look complex. But, with all its past pain, joy, regrets, sin, and insecurities, the soul is being joined to another, who is possibly still in the same state in which they are endeavouring to become one. This is why it is necessary to keep your promise.

Therefore, ask these questions in a way that respects the individual's need for space and privacy:

- "I admire your independence and respect your need for solitude. Can you share what draws you to enjoy time alone?"
- "I sense there might be something on your mind. Is there anything you'd like to talk about or share?"
- "You have a calm presence, and I appreciate that about you. Is there anything you're comfortable discussing, or would you prefer some quiet time?"
- "I've noticed you're more reserved lately. Is there anything you'd like to share, or would you prefer to process things independently?"
- "Your quiet nature is a part of what makes you unique. Is there anything specific you're reflecting on or dealing with internally?"

- "I understand everyone has their own pace and space. Is there anything I can do to support you during this time?"
- "You have a strong sense of independence, and I respect that. Would you feel comfortable sharing anything about your experiences?"
- "I value your privacy and respect your need for personal space. If there's ever anything you want to discuss, I'm here to listen."
- "You are taking some time for yourself lately. Is there anything you'd like to share about what's on your mind?"
- "I admire your quiet demeanour. If there's ever anything you want to talk about, I'm here to listen without judgment."

These questions show understanding and support while acknowledging the individual's desire for solitude and privacy.

However, the above questions, when rephrased, can become more rude and intrusive. Couples need more tact and be enlightened about how important it is to find space within relationships.

- "Why are you always isolating yourself? Don't you have friends, or do you just hate people?"
- "Seriously, what's your problem? You're so closed off. Just spill it already!"

- "Why are you being so quiet all the time? It's annoying. Are you just too scared to speak up?"
- "What's with the silent treatment? Are you going through something or just being a drama queen?"
- "Why are you always so secretive? Do you think you're better than everyone else or just too good to share?"
- "Why are you such a loner? Can't handle being around people, or are you too stuck?"
- "You're always off by yourself. Are you hiding something or just trying to avoid everyone?"
- "Why are you so distant? Can't handle real conversation, or are you too wrapped up in your problems?"
- "Why are you being so antisocial lately? Do you even know how to interact with people?"
- "Why do you always act like you're above everyone else? Can't handle being around people, or are you just.

CHAPTER 5

Family Planning

They agree on a family planning strategy but later change their minds about having children or press the other to adhere to a different timeline.

They agree on a family planning strategy but later change their minds about having children or press the other to adhere to a different timeline.

"I love children and want to have them, but I do not want them; why not? I want them, but not now. Do I feel inadequate to have them? We do not have enough resources to take care of them."

MArk 3:25 KJV "And if a house be divided against itself, that house cannot stand."

BE AWARE OF DIVERGENT VIEWS

"Divergent" connotes ideas, opinions, or paths that vary or contrast. It means something that moves away from a common point or path, indicating a difference or deviation. Where divergence begins to take root, couples will be tempted not to keep promises.

Divergent views on family planning can profoundly impact the dynamics of a relationship, potentially leading to dissatisfaction and discord over time. When partners hold differing opinions on the number of children, timing of pregnancies, or methods of contraception, it can create significant tension within the relationship.

Communication breakdown often accompanies these differences as couples struggle to openly discuss and reconcile their views. This lack of communication can fuel misunderstandings, frustrations, and emotional distance between partners, undermining the foundation of trust and intimacy. Additionally, unmet expectations regarding family planning can breed disappointment and disillusionment, further contributing to dissatisfaction in the relationship.

Furthermore, the communication breakdown can extend beyond practical matters and affect the couple's prayer life. When partners feel disconnected or unresolved about essential issues such as family planning, they may struggle to come together in prayer. This disruption in spiritual unity can leave the couple vulnerable to unwanted spiritual attacks, further exacerbating the strain on the relationship.

In such challenging times, seeking professional and pastoral guidance can provide invaluable support and perspective. Trusted counsellors or spiritual advisors can offer insight, advice, and tools for navigating differences in family planning while fostering open communication and understanding between partners. Moreover, couples can find strength and clarity through prayer, recognizing that God is the owner of life and the giver of children. Honouring His will and seeking His guidance in family planning matters can help couples align their decisions with His purpose and find peace in their journey together. (Psalms 127:3)

The stress and resentment arising from conflicting family planning preferences can affect both partners' well-being. Feelings of pressure to conform to a partner's desires or compromise on deeply held beliefs can lead to emotional strain and mental anguish. This strain can extend to the realm of intimacy, as concerns about unplanned pregnancies or disagreements over contraception methods may dampen sexual connection and emotional intimacy.

Moreover, divergent views on family planning can influence decision-making dynamics within the relationship, affecting choices related to career, finances, and personal aspirations. Conflicting goals in these areas can exacerbate feelings of resentment and compromise, impacting overall satisfaction with the relationship.

In the long run, unresolved differences in family planning can have lasting implications for the stability and happiness of the relationship. If there are children involved, it might start corroding your parental obligations. Persistent dissatisfaction and discord may contribute to emotional distress, mental health issues, or even the breakdown of the relationship. Unaddressed conflicts related to family planning can hinder personal growth, limit shared experiences, and erode the overall quality of life for both partners.

To navigate these challenges and foster a supportive and fulfilling partnership, couples must prioritize effective communication, mutual respect, and willingness to compromise. Proactively addressing concerns, seeking professional guidance and pastoral counsel, and working together to find common ground are essential steps toward building a resilient and mutually satisfying relationship.

While divergent views on family planning can present significant challenges, couples who approach these differences with understanding, empathy, and a shared commitment to growth are better equipped to overcome obstacles and cultivate a thriving relationship built on trust, respect, and mutual fulfilment.

Additionally, we'll explore how a perspective centred on the blessing of having a family, particularly from a Christian standpoint, can guide couples in responsibly navigating changes in family planning decisions while prioritizing each other's happiness.

INITIAL AGREEMENT ON FAMILY PLANNING

At the beginning of a relationship or marriage, couples often discuss and agree upon their family planning goals, including the desired number of children and the timeline for starting a family. These agreements are made with the understanding that both partners are aligned in their vision for the future and are committed to supporting each other's wishes.

CHANGING PREFERENCES OR CIRCUMSTANCES

Over time, individuals may undergo personal growth, experiences, or changes in circumstances that cause them to reassess their family planning goals. One partner may realize they no longer desire children due to career aspirations, health concerns, or other personal reasons. Alternatively, unexpected challenges or opportunities may arise that prompt a reevaluation of the agreed-upon timeline for starting a family.

PRESSURE AND EXPECTATIONS

If one partner experiences a shift in their family planning preferences, they may struggle to communicate this change to their partner. Fear of disappointing or upsetting their partner, coupled with societal expectations surrounding marriage and family, can lead to feelings of guilt or pressure to conform to the initial agreement.

IMPACT ON RELATIONSHIP DYNAMICS

Failure to openly and honestly address changes in family planning goals can strain the relationship and erode trust. Resentment may build if one partner feels pressured or coerced into adhering to the original agreement despite their changed preferences. A lack of mutual understanding and flexibility in adapting to evolving circumstances can create tension and conflict within the relationship.

POPULATION TRENDS IN EUROPE

In many European countries, declining birth rates and ageing populations have become significant demographic challenges. Factors contributing to these trends include changing social norms, economic pressures, and lifestyle choices prioritizing career and personal fulfilment over starting a family. Couples' reluctance or inability to adapt their family planning decisions to evolving circumstances also contributes to these population declines.

CHRISTIAN PERSPECTIVE ON FAMILY BLESSINGS

From a Christian standpoint, the family is considered a sacred institution and a source of blessing and fulfilment. While the decision to have children is deeply personal, it should be guided by principles of love, selflessness, and responsibility towards future generations. Christian couples have the wisdom to prioritize each other's happiness and well-being while discerning God's will for their family and future generations.

TAKING RESPONSIBILITY FOR HAPPINESS:

When making changes in family planning decisions, Christian couples are encouraged to prioritize open communication, mutual respect, and empathy for each other's desires and concerns. Through active listening, you will learn to capture each other perspective with loving accuracy as you seek guidance through prayer and reflection and make decisions that are rooted in love and a shared commitment to each other's happiness.

FLEXIBILITY AND ADAPTABILITY

Recognizing that family planning is a dynamic and evolving process, do not become pressured in your decision. Like other couples, Christian couples approach changes in their desires or circumstances with humility because they trust in God and, "yes", trust in God's providence. This may involve reevaluating previously made agreements in light of new insights or challenges and being open to adjusting plans accordingly while remaining grounded in faith and mutual love.

In conclusion, sensitivity to keeping promises regarding family planning is crucial for maintaining trust and harmony in relationships while acknowledging God, the blesser, and The blessings and responsibilities associated with starting a family. By approaching family planning decisions with open communication, mutual respect, and a shared commitment to each other's happiness, couples can navigate changes in their desires or circumstances while remaining rooted in love and faith.

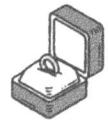

CHAPTER 6

Lifestyle Changes

They promise to adopt certain lifestyle changes (e.g., quitting smoking, exercising regularly) but fail to follow through.

They promise to adopt certain lifestyle changes (e.g., quitting smoking, exercising regularly) but fail to follow through.

Lifestyle changes are the most visible and measurable when we refer to promises. They include visible progress and commitment levels, such as quitting smoking, exercising regularly, or eating healthier. However, these promises are also prone to being disregarded when people feel a win on the wedding day, which can exert a lot of pressure on relationships! Such promises can create significant pressure when not followed through, particularly when one partner fails to follow through on their commitment.

I have also seen cases where individuals desire the relationship so intensely that throughout the counselling period, they were submissive and complied with all appointments, even making seemingly positive adjustments and promises to adapt to future demands. On the surface, the individual was committed to keeping this promise of adjustment. Still, even on the wedding day, it was apparent that this couple was heading for disaster.

Do not allow the excitement of the moment, the enthusiastic comments of peers, and the wishes of your family and friends to overshadow the efforts required to make certain adjustments or wait for your partner to make certain adjustments before proceeding.

They say that patience is a virtue, and I concur. In this case, where you will make a life-altering decision, taking a brief time out is only wise. You never know. During that rest period, individuals have a way of reflecting and gaining perspective on the severity of the situation. You may positively assist your beloved, by your brief absence or separation as the case may be, to figure things out, get their mind straight, and make the necessary changes through the decision they make for themselves rather than falling head over heels due to pressure.

Remember that habits are built over a long period and will not drastically improve because of a wedding date. You need a more profound desire to improve your life from your heart, dependent on your newfound love and determined or driven by your commitment to living a far more disciplined and successful life.

A lifestyle change is a promise that your spouse can already measure; therefore, it can become a source of frustration from the early stages of your marriage. The objections could begin with simple loving statements like "Did you forget what you promised? Are you working on it?" and escalate to more probing and attacking comments. This process can escalate depending on the other's patience.

That is why the scripture warns against being unequally yoked. From the perspective of the promise of a lifestyle change, being equally yoked can play to a couple's advantage. At least great understanding and grace will be given, but the challenge comes when they are unequally yoked. Are you equally or unequally yoked in values?

If you value the concept of being unequally yoked, it's essential to approach these promises cautiously and take them seriously.

Here are some reasons why:

1. **Unequal Yoking and Shared Values**: The concept of being unequally yoked, often referenced in Christian teachings, highlights the importance of shared values, beliefs, and lifestyle choices in a relationship. When one partner commits to making positive lifestyle changes, such as quitting smoking, getting a job, leaving bad company or adopting healthier habits, both partners need to be aligned in their commitment to support and encourage each other in achieving these goals. If one partner consistently fails to uphold their end of the commitment, it can create a sense of imbalance and discord in the relationship.
2. **Trust and Accountability**: Promises to make lifestyle changes require trust and accountability between partners. Trust can be eroded when one partner repeatedly fails to follow through on their commitments, leading to disappointment, resentment, and even anger. Trust is the foundation of a healthy relationship, and when broken promises compromise it, it can strain the bond between partners and undermine the relationship's overall health.
3. **Impact on Health and Well-being**: The decision to make lifestyle changes such as quitting smoking or exercising regularly is very tempting, especially by enthusiastic partners, to please the other or keep the moments interesting, but the

promise of health and well-being can impact relationships immensely. When a partner makes such promises, it must be pursued wholeheartedly, with the utmost vigour, to keep their part of the promise. Failing to follow through on these commitments can have severe consequences for both partners' spiritual, physical and emotional health. It's essential to recognize the importance of prioritizing one's health and taking proactive steps to make positive changes, even if it requires effort and sacrifice.

4. **Red Flags and Reevaluation**: When one partner repeatedly fails to uphold their promises regarding lifestyle changes, it can serve as a red flag indicating underlying issues within the relationship. It's worth taking such moments of doubt seriously and considering whether the relationship is genuinely compatible regarding values, goals, and priorities. Suppose a partner's unwillingness to change or lack of commitment to shared goals becomes a recurring issue. In that case, it may be necessary to reevaluate the relationship and consider whether it's worth continuing.

5. **Self-Reflection and Growth**: Addressing challenges related to broken promises requires self-reflection and a willingness to confront uncomfortable truths. Both partners must be willing to take responsibility for their actions,

communicate their concerns and feelings openly, and make a concerted effort to work towards positive change. This process of self-reflection and growth can strengthen the relationship and deepen the bond between partners, provided both are committed to honest communication and mutual respect.

In conclusion, promises to make lifestyle changes should be taken seriously in relationships, particularly from the perspective of being unequally yoked and the importance of shared values and commitments.

When one partner consistently fails to follow through on their promises, it's essential to approach the situation cautiously and consider whether the relationship is compatible regarding goals and priorities.

Open communication through counselling, trust, and a shared commitment to personal growth and well-being are essential for navigating challenges and making godly decisions.

CHAPTER 7

Communication

Vowing always to communicate openly and honestly but later resorting to lies or omissions to avoid conflict.

Vowing always to communicate openly and honestly but later resorting to lies or omissions to avoid conflict.

"Man is least himself when he talks in his person. Give him a mask, and he will tell you the truth." - Oscar Wilde.

Vowing to communicate openly and honestly but later resorting to deflections, lies, or omissions to avoid conflict can severely undermine the foundation of a healthy relationship. Drawing this wisdom from scripture, I have often been taught that lying or not being fully honest is human (Numbers 23:19) because we do not have all the truth.

That is why I always advise couples to start their communication lives in a relationship with trusted Christian counselling. It helps them grow with each other in a safe environment that allows for honest heart-to-heart conversation, a discipline that will be a powerful asset for future growth.

One blessing of counselling is that it facilitates the couple's unlearning process of what they have learned about verbal and non-verbal communication. Much of what we have learned about communication is clouded by what we learn from a worldly standpoint, which involves body language associated with flirting, subliminal messaging, and often manipulating another's feelings.

In the kingdom of God, however, communication is vastly different. Currently, couples are usually in deep water, and questions may arise regarding what godly communication is and is not. We need wisdom, understanding, patience, mercy, and all these spiritual virtues to mature in communication.

Secondly, in counselling, we will relearn God's ways of communication, how to be bold enough to speak the truth in love, how to be unreserved, knowing that it is only beneficial to both and that it takes that to walk in total healing and deliverance. We can also share our feelings without fear of being shut down.

Thirdly, in counselling, you learn the art of active and godly listening, where we listen with the motive to truly hear the other's heart, keeping in mind that in doing so, we will facilitate both couples' healing process. These are potent gems that counselling can deliver to couples seeking to enter into marriage. I have seen couples in counselling light up and initiate rich conversation when they realize that communication can be holy and helpful, that it is not all about being alluring, sexy, or manipulative and that God has provided other safer spiritual rooms where dialogue can be effective, secure and held with deep regards to their feelings.

They light up, seeing that someone is listening deeply. People will take the lying route when they have not learned the art and science of communicating from the heart, a lesson only God, through wisdom, can deliver to the couple.

Otherwise, they will begin to fail in holding you to their promises and their views when they feel threatened and attacked. When they think of taking the easier route of silence and pretence to evade arguments or quarrels, they fail in this promise to always share their feelings because they conclude that others cannot understand or see their standpoint on a matter.

Here's a deeper exploration of this premise, emphasizing the non-negotiable importance of good communication, the value of pre-marital counselling, and the wisdom and blessings it can offer:

NON-NEGOTIABLE IMPORTANCE OF GOOD COMMUNICATION

Open and honest communication is the cornerstone of a healthy and thriving relationship, especially from a perspective that values relationships before God. When couples vow to communicate openly and honestly, they commit to fostering trust, understanding, and intimacy. It was Bishop George Bloomer who coined the phrase "intimacy means in-to-me-see". There are moments in counselling where we can unknowingly allow one couple to claim to be more passive, shy, and or introverted. In a sense, it can be accurate, but such individuals should be encouraged to start developing skills that will aid in them opening up. I will caution the intended couples when communication breaks down due to lies or omissions; it erodes trust and creates barriers to true intimacy and connection.

IMPACT OF LIES AND OMISSIONS

Lies and omissions in communication can have far-reaching consequences in a relationship. They breed mistrust and suspicion between partners, leading to betrayal and resentment. Moreover, avoiding conflict through dishonesty only postpones and exacerbates the underlying issues, making resolution more challenging in the long run. From a Christian perspective, honesty and integrity are essential virtues that honour God and strengthen the bonds of love and commitment in a relationship.

VALUE OF PRE-MARITAL COUNSELING

Pre-marital counselling offers couples an invaluable opportunity to lay a strong foundation for their future together. Through guided discussions and exercises, couples can explore essential topics such as communication, conflict resolution, shared values, and expectations for marriage. Pre-marital counselling provides a safe space for couples to address potential challenges and develop healthy communication strategies before they become entrenched patterns in the relationship.

WISDOM AND BLESSINGS OF COUNSELING

Seeking counselling before marriage allows couples to benefit from the wisdom and insights of a trained professional or mentor who can offer guidance and support. A third, mature voice can provide perspective, challenge unhealthy patterns, and help couples navigate difficult conversations with grace and understanding. By addressing communication issues early on, couples can build a robust, resilient relationship that honours God and reflects His love and truth.

COUNSELLING AS A SOURCE OF STRENGTH

Rather than viewing counselling as a sign of weakness or failure, couples should see it as a proactive step towards building a healthy and fulfilling relationship. Counselling offers couples tools and strategies to communicate effectively, resolve conflicts constructively, and deepen their emotional connection. Through prayer, reflection, and counselling, couples can cultivate humility, patience, and empathy in their communication, allowing God's wisdom and blessings to guide their relationship.

In summary, good communication is non-negotiable to developing a healthy relationship with God. Lies and omissions undermine trust and intimacy, while pre-marital counselling provides couples with the opportunity to address communication issues and build a strong foundation for their future together. By seeking guidance and support from wise counsellors and mentors, couples can navigate challenges, grow in love and understanding, and honour God in their relationship.

CHAPTER 8

Support During Tough Times

Promising unwavering support during difficult times but later withdrawing emotionally or physically when faced with challenges.

Promising unwavering support during difficult times but later withdrawing emotionally or physically when faced with challenges.

Promising unwavering support during tough times and withdrawing emotionally or physically when faced with challenges can deeply hurt the foundation of a relationship. It's essential to recognize that challenges are a part of life, and unexpected, even deadly, events can occur at any time. Here's a deeper dive into why challenges are inevitable and how personal development and mutual support can serve as anchors through tough times:

INEVITABILITY OF CHALLENGES

Challenges are an inherent part of the human experience. Whether they come from health issues, financial struggles, loss of loved ones, or unforeseen crises, no one is immune to life's difficulties. Recognizing and accepting this reality is the first step towards building resilience and grit in adversity.

APPRECIATING GROWTH

Instead of viewing challenges as solely negative experiences, couples can reframe them as opportunities for growth and learning. Each challenge presents a chance to strengthen one's character, deepen one's relationship with one's partner, and cultivate resilience in the face of hardship. By appreciating and supporting each other's growth through tough times, couples can emerge more robust and more bonded than before.

PERSONAL DEVELOPMENT

Investing in personal development is essential for building emotional, mental, and spiritual fortitude to sustain individuals and couples through pleasant and challenging times. The couple may become intentional and get involved in the unset with training to develop practical skills from Christian therapy, counselling, mindfulness, spiritual reflection, and ongoing learning. By prioritizing personal growth, one should not wait when things are getting tense and storming between you, but you should add all these skill development programs as part of your leisure time. Couples tend to check their developmental lists on rainy days; it is running to shop for the extinguisher when your Home is already in flames.

Couples are encouraged to prioritize reading books, meditating on scriptures, praying together, enjoying times of worship, and attending church. All these add up to developing the inner strength and resilience needed to navigate life's challenges with grace and courage.

MUTUAL SUPPORT AND CONTRIBUTION

In marriage, offering unwavering support means being there for your partner in good times, hardships, and uncertainties. Mutual support is a promise that most may not realize when it slips, but stay on top by being empathetic, active listeners, and willing to offer practical assistance and emotional comfort when needed. It is as simple as providing your partner with their favourite beverage, all they may need to break down and feel loved. The big things are essential, but minor things can steal precious moments. Couples can strengthen their bond by actively contributing to each other's growth and well-being through encouragement, affirmation, or assistance in overcoming challenges. Remember that to make a withdrawal, you may have invested.

COMMUNICATION AND VULNERABILITY

Open and honest communication is critical to providing practical support during tough times. Couples should feel comfortable expressing their fears, concerns, and needs to each other without fear of judgment or rejection. Vulnerability fosters intimacy and connection, allowing couples to weather storms together with mutual understanding and compassion.

CULTIVATING RESILIENCE TOGETHER

Facing challenges as a team can strengthen the bond between partners and deepen their sense of unity and shared purpose. Couples can draw strength from each other's presence and commitment by cultivating resilience together, knowing they have a supportive partner through life's ups and downs.

In summary, challenges are an inevitable part of life, but how couples navigate them can profoundly impact the strength and longevity of their relationship. By investing in personal development, appreciating each other's growth, and offering unwavering support through tough times, couples can build emotional, mental, and spiritual fortitude as a solid anchor in the face of life's uncertainties. Together, they can weather any storm and emerge more robust, connected, and resilient than ever.

CHAPTER 9

Respecting Boundaries

They agree to respect each other's boundaries but later cross them without consent.

They agree to respect each other's boundaries but later cross them without consent.

God is a God of boundaries!

Here are some cautions worth noting: maintaining this beautiful promise to honour boundaries can be a powerful tool for a source of dream inspiration and activation of spiritual giftings within the marriage covenant. Boundaries are of God, and there is a spiritual pocket reserved for His Spirit with us even when we decide to be married.

The scripture alerts us to the need for abstinence for fasting and prayers, a time for spiritual reflection, and a time to receive guidance for your family. Remember that God blesses both couples, and they both have a divine purpose to fulfil within the marriage. The honour and respect of boundaries within this familiar unit will infuse fresh spiritual vitality into your union. (1 Corinthians 7:5)

There is something when a couple can genuinely understand and utilize quiet moments and even find the maturity and trust to encourage this once in a while because a moment with God can amount to years of joy and bliss in your Home.

Ecclesiastes 4:11-12 NKJVAgain, if two lie down together, they will keep warm; But how can one be warm *alone?* Though one may be overpowered by another, two can withstand him. And a threefold cord is not quickly broken.

This promise invokes spirit because God is the third person in your marriage. His spirit is the glue, seeing that marriage was His idea in the first place. He brought Adam and Eve to the altar, as it were, and performed the first wedding in the Garden of Eden. The threefold brings to light the need for the consistent work of the supernatural within every marriage. If a lack of such, a marriage will soon become fragmented. Where it may seem nice to make this promise of boundary, it is wise to take this to heart and sensitize both hearts to understand and facilitate the moment intimacy with God. The scripture reveals that, indeed, two can withstand a lot of challenges. Still, it quickly refers to the reality of the third cord, which brings a power dimension to this unit that causes it to be unbroken.

How can an overly close claim of personal interest contribute to the fragmentation of spiritual boundaries:

1. **Desensitization to Feelings and Desires**: Couples may become desensitized to each other's feelings and spiritual desires, particularly if they become overly familiar or comfortable in the relationship. This desensitization can lead to a lack of empathy toward each other spiritual needs and consideration for each other's boundaries, as partners may assume they already know what the other person wants or needs without actively seeking consent or understanding what God is doing in each other.
2. **Shielding Our Bowels of Compassion**: An overly close claim of personal interest in the relationship can create a sense of entitlement or ownership over the other person, leading to a disregard for their boundaries and individuality. Do you know that in marriage, the fastest way to lose Intimacy with God is when you

hinder your partner's intimacy with the Father? When one partner prioritizes their needs and desires above their partner's and that of the Holy Spirit, it can result in a lack of compassion and empathy, further exacerbating boundary violations.

3. **Productivity and Growth**: Respecting boundaries is essential for maintaining a healthy relationship and fostering individual productivity and growth. Boundaries provide a framework for personal autonomy and self-care, allowing individuals to prioritize their needs, interests, and goals, especially in the spiritual aspect of their lives. When boundaries are respected, individuals feel empowered to pursue their passions and aspirations, leading to greater personal and spiritual fulfilment. In reality, married couples are supposed to be excited and experience a great measure of the power that flows from the presence of The Holy Spirit because, as the word said, the two should become one. Jesus declared in Matthew 18:19 - 20 KJV Again I say unto you, That if two of you shall agree on earth as touching any thing that they shall ask, it shall be done for them of my Father which is in heaven. As you have already worked out, marriage is where you find the closest individuals who can unite in prayer and tremendous power.

4. **Different Types of Boundaries**: Boundaries in relationships extend beyond physical space and encompass various aspects of personal, emotional, and psychological well-being. Some examples of boundaries that may be overlooked include:
   - Emotional Boundaries: Respect each other's feelings, opinions, and emotional needs without judgment or criticism.
   - Time Boundaries: Allowing each other space and time for individual pursuits, hobbies, and interests without constantly feeling obligated to be together.
   - Communication Boundaries: Listening actively and attentively to each other's concerns, thoughts, and feelings without interrupting or dismissing them.
   - Privacy Boundaries: Respect each other's privacy and autonomy in personal matters, such as phone conversations, social media use, and personal space.
   - Financial Boundaries: Agreeing on economic decisions and respecting each other's financial goals, spending habits, and boundaries related to money management.

Let's review the earlier discussion. A relationship's promise to respect boundaries can be destroyed when partners become desensitized to each other's feelings and desires, disregarding personal autonomy and mutual respect. An overly close claim of personal interest can contribute to boundary violations by prioritizing one's needs above those of the partner. However, by recognizing the importance of boundaries in fostering productivity, growth, and mutual respect, couples can work together to create a healthier and more fulfilling relationship.

CHAPTER 10

Shared Goals

We agreed on shared long-term goals but later pursued individual interests without considering the relationship.

We agreed on shared long-term goals but later pursued individual interests without considering the relationship.

Couples with a healthy Christian relationship and shared goals often exhibit several vital characteristics. One is that their relationship is rooted in a shared faith in God, with both partners committed to living according to Christian values and principles. They prioritize prayer, worship, and spiritual growth both individually and together.

Secondly, they have a clear vision for their relationship that aligns with their Christian values. They set shared goals for their spiritual growth, family life, career, and service to others based on biblical principles and pursue them with unity and purpose.The biblical understanding of marriage emphasizes the concept of two individuals becoming one in a profoundly intimate and committed union. This union is physical and encompasses emotional, spiritual, and relational aspects.

When couples vow to share long-term goals, they commit to aligning their aspirations, dreams, and plans for the future in a unified manner. However, when individual interests take precedence over the shared goals of the relationship, it can lead to discord and fragmentation within the marriage.

The process of truly becoming one with another person is multifaceted and requires a foundation of healing, growth, and mutual understanding. Here's a closer look at how past pain, regrets, and fears can influence the journey toward oneness in marriage:

1. **Healing from Past Pain**: Many individuals bring emotional baggage and wounds from past experiences into their relationships. Unresolved trauma, hurtful memories, and unhealed wounds can hinder the process of becoming one with a partner. Healing from past pain requires courage, vulnerability, and

a willingness to confront and address unresolved issues. Couples committed to supporting each other's healing journey can create a safe and nurturing environment for growth and transformation.
2. **Overcoming Regrets and Resentments**: Regrets and resentments from past mistakes or conflicts can create barriers to intimacy and connection in marriage. Holding onto grudges or dwelling on past failures can prevent couples from fully embracing the present moment and working towards shared goals. Forgiveness, empathy, and grace are essential for overcoming regrets and resentments and fostering a spirit of reconciliation and renewal within the relationship.
3. **Conquering Fears and Insecurities**: Fear of vulnerability, rejection, or failure can sabotage efforts to become one with a partner. Due to underlying insecurities or anxieties, individuals may hesitate to invest in the relationship or fully pursue shared goals. Building trust, open communication, and a supportive atmosphere of acceptance and love can help partners overcome their fears and insecurities, allowing them to embrace the journey of oneness with confidence and courage.
4. **Commitment to Growth and Transformation**: Ultimately, becoming one with another person is an ongoing journey of growth and

transformation. It requires a deep commitment to personal and relational development and a willingness to adapt, compromise, and learn from each other. Couples who prioritize mutual respect, empathy, and communication can navigate the challenges and complexities of marriage with grace and resilience, emerging more robust and united than before.

Furthermore, when neglected, pain, regrets, and fear will create a self-centred heart prone to self-preservation. Shared goals and promises are not for the person who is hurt. Self-centeredness can significantly negatively impact shared goals within a relationship, particularly in a Christian relationship where the emphasis is often on mutual love, service, and sacrifice. Here's how self-centeredness can affect shared goals:

Self-centeredness can profoundly impact shared goals, particularly in a Christian partnership. When individuals prioritize their own needs, desires, and ambitions over those of their partner or the shared goals of the relationship, this leads to a lack of alignment in priorities and values. This misalignment makes it challenging to work towards common objectives, as limited collaboration ensues.

Self-centred individuals may be unwilling to compromise or collaborate, insisting on having things their way or pursuing personal agendas. This behaviour undermines the unity and cooperation necessary for achieving common goals. Moreover, self-centeredness often diminishes support for a partner's aspirations and endeavours, with individuals being critical, dismissive, or indifferent towards their partner's goals. Ultimately, this undermines the foundation of a healthy, mutually fulfilling relationship and impedes progress towards shared goals. Conversely, prioritizing selflessness, empathy, and mutual respect fosters unity, collaboration, and the achievement of shared objectives in a Christian relationship.

Self-centeredness undermines the foundation of a healthy, mutually fulfilling relationship and can impede progress towards shared goals. In contrast, prioritizing selflessness, empathy, and mutual respect fosters unity, collaboration, and, ultimately, achieving shared objectives in a Christian relationship.

In summary, the biblical understanding of marriage emphasizes the profound unity and intimacy that occurs when two individuals become one in a committed relationship. However, achieving this oneness requires a foundation of healing, growth, and mutual understanding. By addressing past pain, regrets, and fears with courage and vulnerability, couples can embark on a journey of transformation that leads to deeper intimacy, shared goals, and a flourishing marriage.

Epilogue

A BRIEF INSIGHT ON INTIMACY

What is Intimacy? I would quote Bishop George Bloomer when He says intimacy is in-to-me-see. From the scriptures, looking into the first relationship of Adam and Eve, the Bible says "that the man and his wife were both naked and were not embarrassed or ashamed in each other's presence. Gen 2:25.

Intimacy involves fostering a relationship characterized by transparency, wherein couples feel secure in expressing their thoughts and emotions without fear of exploitation. Rather than being weaponized against one another, these expressions should be embraced as opportunities for mutual understanding, growth, and transformation. Intimacy entails acknowledging each other's humanity and providing unwavering support through every stage of life, nurturing each other's strengths, talents, and gifts."

Intimacy thrives on the deliberate use of words imbued with virtue. Employing godly language is essential in nurturing relationships, as words possess the power to either uplift or undermine. Negative expressions such as 'You always do things like this or that' fail to acknowledge the nuances of behaviour and breed misunderstanding. Similarly, phrases like 'You do not understand what you are doing' or 'I told you so' only serve to belittle and erode trust. We must purposefully speak kindness and affirmation to cultivate goodness in our relationships.

Over time, the familiarity of living under the same roof can dull the sense of specialness between partners. Simple yet meaningful expressions like 'I love you,' 'You look great,' or 'When did you buy that dress?' may seem unnecessary to married couples, but they play a crucial role in maintaining harmony and affection. Quick phone calls to say 'I love you' serve as reminders of the bond shared. These gestures may be taken for granted, yet they are vital for nurturing peace and love within the marital union."

Intimacy entails a willingness to be receptive to one another, free from self-centeredness or selfishness. Using possessive language such as 'This is my car,' 'this is my house,' or 'this is my account' can lead to unhappiness and loneliness. It is prudent for one spouse to strive for a slightly higher income, fostering an environment of openness and acceptance. Adopting that everything is shared because of the unity forged in marriage is essential in cultivating intimacy and mutual understanding."

Intimacy involves empathizing with the other person's perspective. The insistence on asserting right and wrong within a relationship can often be the root cause of many problems in a marriage. It is imperative to acknowledge that while our viewpoints may be valid, it is equally important to understand and empathize with our spouse's perspective to foster intimacy.

www.ingramcontent.com/pod-product-compliance
Lightning Source LLC
LaVergne TN
LVHW061557070526
838199LV00077B/7087